B♭ Trumpet/Cornet—Book 1 **SECOND EDITION**

Tradition of Excellence™
Comprehensive Band Method
by **Bruce Pearson** & **Ryan Nowlin**

Dear Student:

Welcome to your study of the trumpet or cornet—an exciting adventure filled with rewards and challenges. Through careful study and regular practice, you will quickly discover the joy and satisfaction of playing beautiful music for yourself, your family, your friends, or a concert audience. We wish you many rewarding years of trumpet or cornet playing.

Bruce Pearson Bruce Pearson   *Ryan Nowlin* signature Ryan Nowlin

PRACTICE JOURNAL

Week	Date Assigned	Assignment/Goal	Minutes Practiced							Total Minutes	Initial
			Su	M	Tu	W	Th	F	Sa		
1											
2											
3											
4											
5											
6											
7											
8											
9											
10											
11											
12											
13											
14											
15											
16											

A full Practice Journal is available from your teacher or from your **INTERACTIVE Practice Studio**.

 Enhance your practice by frequently visiting the **INTERACTIVE Practice Studio**. See the inside back cover for more information.

 ***Tradition of Excellence*** is available in SmartMusic. To subscribe, go to www.smartmusic.com.

ISBN 10: 0-8497-7060-2 • ISBN 13: 978-0-8497-7060-9

©2010, 2016 Kjos Music Press, Neil A. Kjos Music Company, Distributor, 4382 Jutland Drive, San Diego, California, 92117.
International copyright secured. All rights reserved. Printed in U.S.A.

 Tradition of Excellence and **INTERACTIVE Practice Studio** are trademarks of Kjos Music Press.

GETTING STARTED

For more detailed instruction, be sure to view the Video Lessons in your *Tradition of Excellence* **INTERACTIVE Practice Studio**. Lessons are available every time you see this icon.

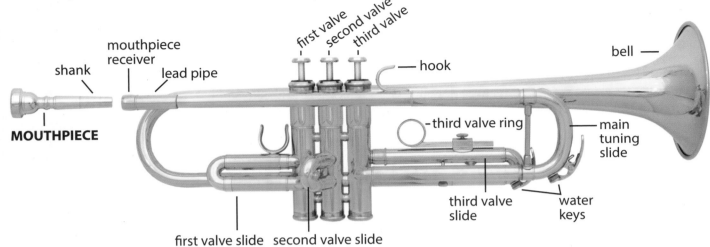

shank

mouthpiece receiver

lead pipe

first valve

second valve

third valve

hook

bell

MOUTHPIECE

third valve ring

main tuning slide

first valve slide   second valve slide

third valve slide

water keys

Assembly

1) Insert the mouthpiece into the receiver on the lead pipe.
2) Gently twist the mouthpiece into place, but not too tightly.

Posture & Hand Position

1) Sit up straight at the edge of your chair with your feet flat on the floor.
2) Grasp the trumpet with your left hand, placing your fingers around the casing of the third valve and your thumb around the casing of the first valve. Place either your ring finger or middle finger of your left hand in the third valve ring.
3) Place the tip of your right thumb under the lead pipe between the first and second valves.
4) Place the tips of the first three fingers of your right hand on the valve buttons. Your right hand should form a relaxed "C," as if holding a tennis ball.
5) Rest your right little finger on top of the hook (not in the hook). Keeping both wrists straight, tilt the instrument slightly to the right. Keep your elbows away from your body.

Forming an Embouchure & Making a Tone

1) Moisten your lips and shape the inside of your mouth and throat as if you are saying "oh." Bring your lips together as if saying "em."
2) Take a full breath of air through your mouth and blow through closed lips, creating a relaxed buzz.
3) Remove the mouthpiece from the instrument and hold it by the shank. Without using too much pressure, place the mouthpiece over the center of the buzz with equal amounts of the mouthpiece on the upper and lower lip. Use a mirror to check your embouchure.
4) Take a full breath of air through your mouth and play a long, steady buzz.
5) Complete the **Mouthpiece Workout** by watching the video lesson and playing along with the recorded accompaniment (see the inside back cover for details).

Daily Care & Maintenance

Putting the Trumpet Away
1) Depress the water key and blow (not buzz) through the trumpet to empty excess water.
2) Wipe off the trumpet with a soft, clean cloth.
3) Push in all slides, making sure you depress the corresponding valve when moving a slide.
4) Remove the mouthpiece and place it in the case.
5) Place the trumpet in the case with the 2nd valve slide facing up. Latch the case.

Oiling the Valves (Daily)
1) Gently remove only the first valve by unscrewing it at the top of the valve casing (not the valve button). Do not turn the valve or touch any part that is protected by the casing.
2) Apply 4 or 5 drops of valve oil along the metal part of the valve in which there are holes.
3) Insert the valve back into the trumpet, turn the valve button to the right (clockwise) until the valve clicks into place, and screw in the valve at the top of the valve casing.
4) Push the valve button up and down rapidly to work in the valve oil.
5) Repeat this process with valves two and three.

Greasing the Slides (Regularly)
1) To remove the slide, depress the corresponding valve button and pull on the slide. (For the main tuning slide, there is no need to depress any valves.) Only remove one slide at a time.
2) Remove existing grease by wiping the slide with a rag.
3) Apply a generous amount of grease to the slide.
4) Insert the slide back into the trumpet, being sure to depress the corresponding valve button.
5) Keeping the valve depressed, move the slide in and out of the instrument to work in the grease.
6) Push the slide all the way in and wipe off the excess grease with a rag.
7) Return the slide to its original position and repeat with the other slides.

TRUMPET/CORNET & BRASS LESSON

Terms & Symbols

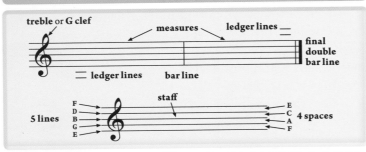

music alphabet – first seven letters of the alphabet; these note names are assigned to the lines and spaces of the staff

Time Signature $\frac{4}{4}$ = number of counts per measure
= type of note (♩) that gets one count

Rhythm

o   **whole note** = 4 counts of sound in $\frac{4}{4}$

▬   **whole rest** = 4 counts of silence in $\frac{4}{4}$

Notes

0 = no valves pressed down

RHYTHM COUNTING

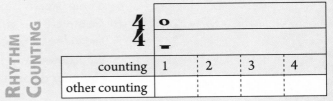

	counting	1	2	3	4
	other counting				

What Do You Hear?

When you play your instrument, you will probably play one of these two notes:

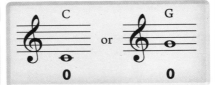

What Next?

Ask your teacher which note you are playing:
If your natural note is C, start on page 4.
If your natural note is G, start on page 5.

Use the audio, video, and extras provided in your *Tradition of Excellence* **INTERACTIVE Practice Studio** to enhance every practice session. See the inside back cover for more information.

staff & bar lines

$\frac{4}{4}$ o ▬

1. The First Note
▶ How is your posture?

2. The Second Note
▶ Extend the 3rd valve slide to play D.
▶ Are you using plenty of air?

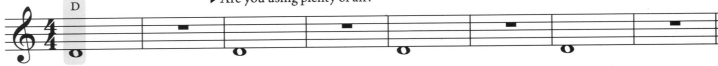

3. Music in Motion
▶ Are you playing with a good embouchure?

4. All Together, Now!
▶ How is your hand position?

5. Mr. Whole Note Takes a Walk
▶ Write the note names beneath the music before you play.

TRUMPET/CORNET & BRASS LESSON

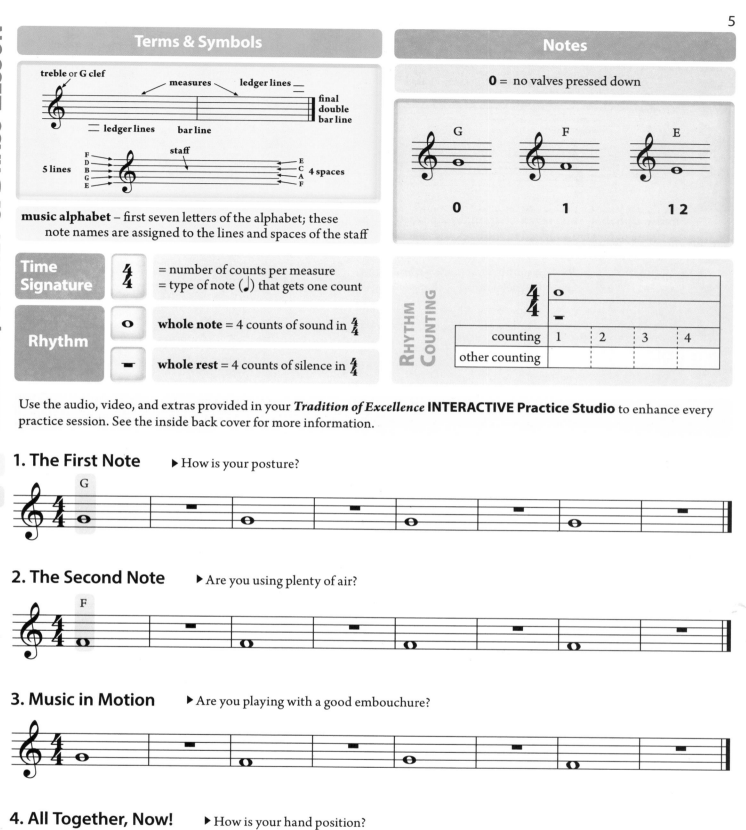

Terms & Symbols

treble or G clef

measures

ledger lines

final double bar line

ledger lines

bar line

staff

5 lines

4 spaces

music alphabet – first seven letters of the alphabet; these note names are assigned to the lines and spaces of the staff

Time Signature

𝄴 = number of counts per measure
= type of note (♩) that gets one count

Rhythm

○ **whole note** = 4 counts of sound in 𝄴

▬ **whole rest** = 4 counts of silence in 𝄴

Notes

0 = no valves pressed down

	G	F	E
	0	1	1 2

RHYTHM COUNTING

𝄴	○			
	▬			
counting	1	2	3	4
other counting				

Use the audio, video, and extras provided in your *Tradition of Excellence* **INTERACTIVE Practice Studio** to enhance every practice session. See the inside back cover for more information.

staff & bar lines

1. The First Note
▶ How is your posture?

(G)

2. The Second Note
▶ Are you using plenty of air?

(F)

3. Music in Motion
▶ Are you playing with a good embouchure?

4. All Together, Now!
▶ How is your hand position?

(E)

5. Mr. Whole Note Takes a Walk
▶ Write the note names beneath the music before you play.

FULL BAND

Terms & Symbols

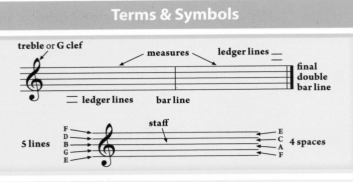

treble or G clef · measures · ledger lines · final double bar line · ledger lines · bar line · staff · 5 lines · 4 spaces

music alphabet – first seven letters of the alphabet; these note names are assigned to the lines and spaces of the staff

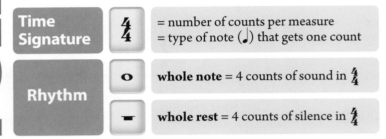

Time Signature 4/4 = number of counts per measure
= type of note (♩) that gets one count

Rhythm
o **whole note** = 4 counts of sound in 4/4
▬ **whole rest** = 4 counts of silence in 4/4

Notes

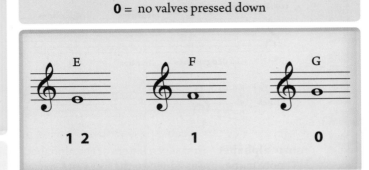

0 = no valves pressed down

E · F · G
1 2 · 1 · 0

COUNTING & CONDUCTING

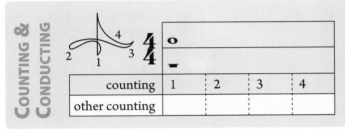

	counting	1	2	3	4
	other counting				

Use the audio, video, and extras provided in your *Tradition of Excellence* **INTERACTIVE Practice Studio** to enhance every practice session. See the inside back cover for more information.

---

staff & bar lines
4/4 o ▬

1. Away We Go!
▸ How is your posture?

2. Going Up?
▸ Are you playing with a steady air stream to produce a smooth, even sound?

3. Count Me In
▸ 1) Write the counting under the music. 2) Clap the rhythm.
3) Sing the notes using "too," the note names, or solfège. 4) Play!

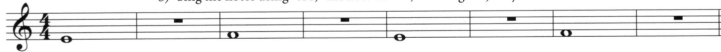

4. Higher Ground
▸ Are you playing with a good embouchure?

5. Moving Around   ✓ TEST
▸ Write the note names beneath the music before you play.

6. Trumpet/Cornet Private Lesson

▸ Here is how to draw a treble clef.   ▸ Draw eight treble clefs on your own. Be sure they circle the second (G) line.

1)   2)

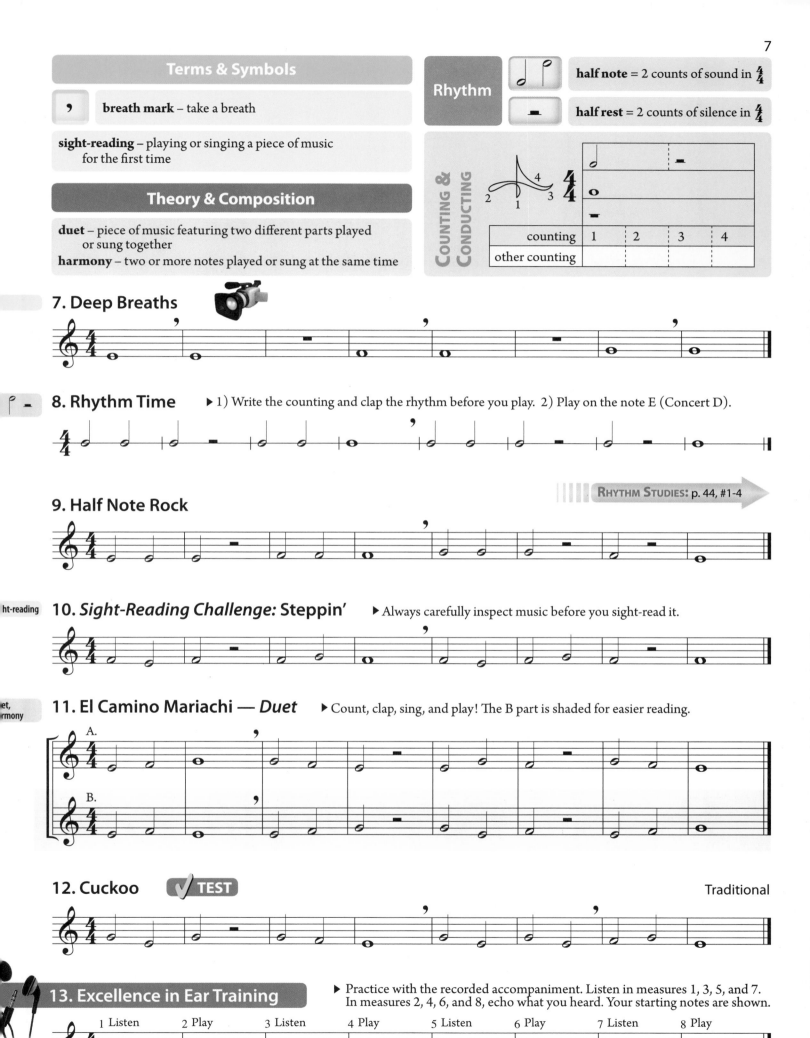

Terms & Symbols

,   **breath mark** – take a breath

sight-reading – playing or singing a piece of music for the first time

Theory & Composition

duet – piece of music featuring two different parts played or sung together

harmony – two or more notes played or sung at the same time

Rhythm

half note = 2 counts of sound in 4/4

half rest = 2 counts of silence in 4/4

COUNTING & CONDUCTING

	counting	1	2	3	4
other counting					

7. Deep Breaths

8. Rhythm Time

▶ 1) Write the counting and clap the rhythm before you play. 2) Play on the note E (Concert D).

9. Half Note Rock

RHYTHM STUDIES: p. 44, #1-4

10. *Sight-Reading Challenge:* Steppin'

▶ Always carefully inspect music before you sight-read it.

11. El Camino Mariachi — *Duet*

▶ Count, clap, sing, and play! The B part is shaded for easier reading.

A.

B.

12. Cuckoo   ✓ TEST

Traditional

13. Excellence in Ear Training

▶ Practice with the recorded accompaniment. Listen in measures 1, 3, 5, and 7. In measures 2, 4, 6, and 8, echo what you heard. Your starting notes are shown.

1 Listen   2 Play   3 Listen   4 Play   5 Listen   6 Play   7 Listen   8 Play

W61TP

Rhythm

quarter note = 1 count of sound in $\frac{4}{4}$

quarter rest = 1 count of silence in $\frac{4}{4}$

COUNTING & CONDUCTING

counting	1	2	3	4
other counting				

Notes

D   C

1 3   0

14. Rhythm Time
▶ 1) Write the counting and clap the rhythm before you play. 2) Play on the note E (Concert D).

RHYTHM STUDIES: p. 44, #5-17

15. Rising Rhythms
▶ Start each note by whispering the word "too."

16. Stepping Stones
▶ Keep the air moving.

17. Rain, Rain
Traditional

18. In a Minor Mood
▶ When playing the note D, extend the 3rd valve slide out about one half inch to play the note in tune. Ask your teacher for help.
▶ Count, clap, sing, and play!

19. Hot Cross Buns
English Folk Song

20. Go Tell Aunt Rhodie ✓ TEST
American Folk Song

21. Trumpet/Cornet Private Lesson
▶ 1) Draw a treble clef at the beginning of the staff.
2) Trace the notes and rests, and draw three more of each.

W61TP

Terms & Symbols

Solo – only one person plays or sings
Soli – a small group or section plays or sings
Tutti – everyone plays or sings

:|| **repeat sign** – play or sing the music again

Time Signature C **common time** = 4/4

Theory & Composition

phrase – musical sentence, often 4 or 8 measures long
round – song in which the same part is played or sung by two or more groups starting at different times
composition – creation of music that can be performed later, usually from written notation

22. Little Robin Redbreast
Traditional

23. Skill Builder: Merrily We Roll Along
▶ Count, clap, sing, and play! When you reach the end of the song, repeat once from the beginning.
Traditional

24. Itsy Bitsy Spider — *Round*
▶ Add brackets to show the phrases.
Traditional

25. A La Rueda
▶ Are you extending the 3rd valve slide on all Ds?
Spanish Folk Song

26. Love Somebody — *Duet*
Traditional

27. Good King Wenceslas ✓ TEST
Traditional English Carol

28. Excellence in Composition
▶ 1) Draw a treble clef. 2) Complete and play your composition.

Title _____   Composer _____

W61TP

Terms & Symbols

articulation – type of attack used to play a note or group of notes

slur – articulation that connects notes of *different* pitches; indicates a very smooth sound with only the first note tongued

one-measure repeat sign – play or sing the previous measure again

Notes

A

1 2

---

slur

29. Warm-up: Serenity — *Round*

▶ Keep the air moving.

30. Chop Builder

▶ Make a clean slur from E to A.

A

%

31. Camptown Races

▶ Draw the missing notes in the ovals before you play.

Stephen Foster, America's first great popular songwriter, was born on the 50th anniversary of American Independence: the Fourth of July, 1826.

Stephen Foster
(1826–1864)
American Composer

Solo/Soli   Tutti   Solo/Soli   Tutti

32. Skill Builder

▶ Add brackets to show the phrases.

33. London Bridge — *Duet*

English Folk Song

A.

B.

34. The Frog's Song — *Round*   ✓ TEST

▶ Are you slurring?

Japanese Folk Song

35. Trumpet/Cornet Private Lesson

▶ Play with a fast and steady air stream.

▶ Repeat this exercise using the following fingerings: 0, 2, 1, 12, 23, 13, 123. Use this as a daily warm-up when you practice. Also play this exercise on your mouthpiece alone.

MASTERING EXCELLENCE: p. 38, #1

Time Signature

²/₄ = two counts per measure
= quarter note gets one count

COUNTING & CONDUCTING

	counting	1	2
	other counting		

Rhythm

tie – marking that connects notes of the *same* pitch to make one longer note

Notes

Key Signature

sharp (♯) or flat (♭) signs placed after a clef

In these key signatures, play or sing:
no sharps or flats | every F as F sharp | every B as B flat | every B as B flat, every E as E flat

36. Rhythm Time   ▶ 1) Write the counting and clap the rhythm before you play. 2) Play on the note D (Concert C).

RHYTHM STUDIES: p. 44, #18-20; p. 46, #41-43

37. Two Step   ▶ The C major (Concert B♭ major) key signature, highlighted in purple, indicates no sharps or flats.

38. *Sight-Reading Challenge:* Shoo Fly   ▶ Are you extending the 3rd valve slide on all Ds?   American Folk Song

39. Russian Folk Song — *Duet*

Beethoven bridged music history's Classical and Romantic Periods.

Ludwig van Beethoven (1770–1827)
German Composer

A.

B.

40. San Serení   ✓ **TEST**   ▶ Add brackets to show the phrases.   Puerto Rican Folk Song

41. Excellence in Theory   ▶ Add the notes and rests together to find the number of counts. A quarter note gets one count.

a)   ♩ + ♩ = ___

b)   ♩ + 𝅗𝅥 = ___

c)   𝄽 + ♩ + ▬ = ___

d)   𝅝 + ▬ = ___

W61TP

ENSEMBLES

Theory & Composition	Terms & Symbols

Theory & Composition

trio – piece of music featuring three different parts played or sung together

introduction – opening passage of a piece of music

theme – a melody within a piece of music

Terms & Symbols

5 | **rehearsal numbers** – find important places in the music using these markers

1. **2.** | **1st and 2nd endings** – play or sing the 1st ending the first time through, repeat, skip the 1st ending, and play or sing the 2nd ending the second time through

𝄐 | **fermata** – hold a note or rest longer than its usual value

Concert Etiquette

—Enter the stage or performance area confidently. Make eye contact with the audience and smile.
—Stand or sit tall. Be positive and energetic. It's fun to share your music with others!

trio,
introduction,
theme

rehearsal
numbers,
1st & 2nd
endings

Solo: A   **Duet:** A + B   **Trio** or **Full Band:** A + B + C

Jingle Bells

J.S. Pierpont (1822–1893)
American Composer

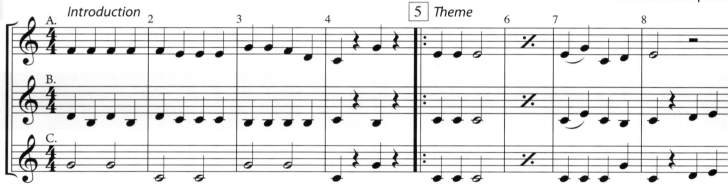

▶ Repeat back to 5 .

Jolly Old St. Nicholas

Traditional

W61TP

The Dreidel Song

Jewish Folk Song

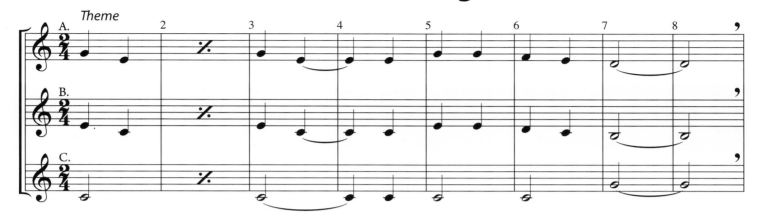

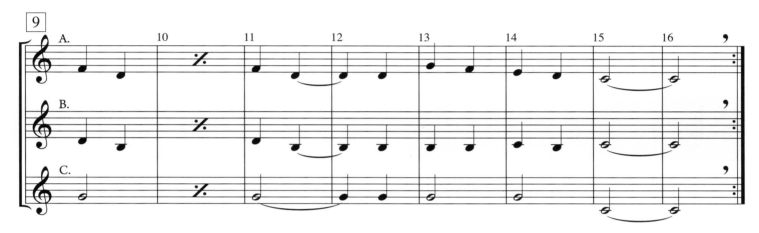

Kwanzaa Celebration

David Bobrowitz (b. 1945)
American Composer

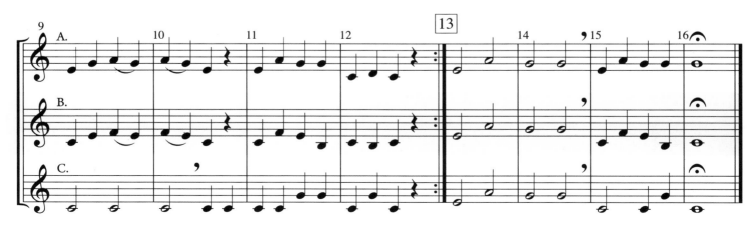

14

W61TP

Theory & Composition   **improvisation** – spontaneous composition of music through playing or singing

49. Unforgettable Eighth Notes

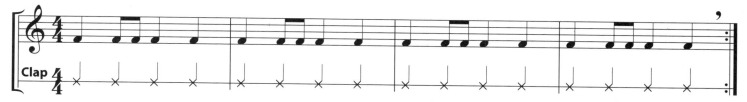

50. Mahnomen Harvest   ▸ Count, clap, sing, and play! Extend the 3rd valve slide to play D.

51. Eighth Notes on the Edge

52. Now Let Me Fly   ▸ Count, clap, sing, and play!

Spirituals are religious folk songs created in the 18th and 19th centuries.

American Spiritual

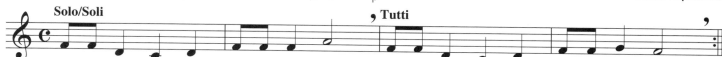

53. *Sight-Reading Challenge:* Promenade   ▸ 1) Write the counting and draw the bar lines. 2) Sight-read!

54. Rio Con Brio   ✓ TEST

55. Excellence in Improvisation   ▸ Play along with the recorded accompaniment. Measures 1-2: Play the written notes. Measures 3-5: Improvise using the same notes.

W61TP

16

Terms & Symbols

accidental – symbol that alters the pitch of a note until the end of the measure

♭ **flat** – lowers the pitch of a note one half step

B → B♭

B
B♭

Notes

B flat (B♭)

1

Rhythm

pick-up or **anacrusis** – music that comes before the first full measure; rhythmic value of the pick-up is sometimes removed from the last measure

Key Signature

F major (Concert E♭ major) – play or sing every B as B♭

Theory & Composition

interval – distance between two pitches
half step – smallest interval used in Western music; on a piano keyboard, it is the distance from one key to the very next key—white or black
theme and variation – type of composition that begins with a main melody (**theme**) and continues with different versions (**variations**) of the main melody

accidental, ♭

56. Warm-up: Chorale — *Duet*

pick-up

57. Rhythm Time
▸ 1) Write the counting and clap the rhythm before you play. 2) Play on the note F (Concert E♭).

RHYTHM STUDIES: p. 45, #21-35; p. 46, #44-46

58. Skill Builder: Boil the Cabbage Down — *Duet*
▸ Circle the notes changed by the key signature in line B.

American Folk Song

theme & variation

59. Bingo Variations ✓ TEST
▸ 1) Play the black notes, which make up the theme.
2) Add the gray notes, which make up the variation.

American Folk Song

60. Trumpet/Cornet Private Lesson
▸ Are you extending the 3rd valve slide on every D?

MASTERING EXCELLENCE: p. 38, #2

18

| Terms & Symbols | tempo – speed of a piece of music
Andante – walking tempo; slower than **Moderato**
Moderato – medium tempo
Allegro – fast tempo | *mp*

mf | *mezzo piano* – medium soft

mezzo forte – medium loud | accent – emphasize the note |

Andante

67. Warm-up: Lullaby

▸ Use plenty of air to sustain each pitch.
▸ Are you extending the 3rd valve slide on every D?

Welsh Folk Song

Allegro

68. Ezekiel Saw the Wheel — *Duet*

American Spiritual

***mp*, >**
Moderato

69. Rhythm Time

▸1) Write the counting and clap the rhythm before you play. 2) Play on the note C (Concert Bb).

RHYTHM STUDIES: p. 46, #54-58

70. *Sight-Reading Challenge:* Streets of Laredo

Laredo is a city in Texas on the Mexican border.

American Folk Song

mf

71. Skill Builder: Donkey Riding

▸ 1) Add brackets to show the phrases.
2) Add a breath mark between the phrases.

Canadian Folk Song

72. Theme from "The Nutcracker" ✓ TEST

Tchaikovsky first studied to be a lawyer but eventually became a full-time composer thanks to the support of a wealthy patron.

Peter Ilyich Tchaikovsky (1840–1893)
Russian Composer

73. Trumpet/Cornet Private Lesson

▸ Increase the tempo slightly each time you practice this exercise. Learning these finger patterns is important to your progress.

MASTERING EXCELLENCE: p. 38, #3

Solo

In addition to his work as a composer and author, Ryan Nowlin is a music teacher, horn player, and singer.

The Good Life
Solo with Piano Accompaniment

Ryan Nowlin (b. 1978)
American Composer

BAND PIECES

Theory & Composition	Terms & Symbols

chord – two or more notes sounded at the same time

closing – last measures of a composition, often containing music added to give a feeling of finality

long rest or **multiple-measure rest** – rest for the number of measures indicated

Concert Etiquette
—If you make a mistake, never let it show. Keep playing or singing as if nothing happened.
—When you are finished, graciously accept the audience's applause. Leave the stage area confidently.

chord

Warm-up: Tone, Balance, and Tuning

▶ There are many ways to perform a warm-up; follow the instructions given by your director.

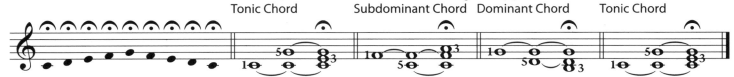

closing

long rest

March Across the Seas

Bruce Pearson (b. 1942) and Ryan Nowlin (b. 1978) American Composers

Bruce Pearson played clarinet and saxophone as well as baseball and hockey into his college years before becoming a music teacher, author, composer, and conductor.

Procession
from "Water Music"

George Frideric Handel (1685–1759) English Composer arr. Ryan Nowlin

Water Music was written for a royal boat party on England's Thames River. The orchestra played from one barge while King George I and friends listened from another vessel close by.

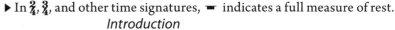

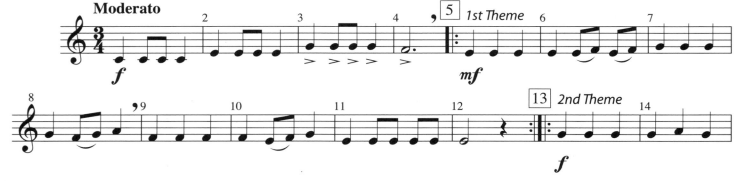

Banana Boat Song

Jamaican Folk Song
arr. Ryan Nowlin

Indigo Rock

Bruce Pearson & Ryan Nowlin
American Composers

Terms & Symbols

crescendo – gradually louder
decrescendo – gradually softer

natural – cancels a flat (♭) or sharp (♯)

divisi (div.) – some performers play or sing the top notes while others play or sing the bottom notes

unisono (unis.) – everyone plays or sings the same notes

Notes

B flat (B♭)

1

74. Warm-up: "Werde munter" — Duet

Andante

Johann Schop was a virtuoso violinist but also played cornet and trombone. This melody by Schop was used by J.S. Bach in his famous **Cantata 147**.

Johann Schop (1590–1667)
German Composer

75. Fais Dodo

▸ Are you extending the 3rd valve slide on every D?

French Folk Song

Andante

76. Baroque March

Though considered an English composer, Handel was born in Germany.

George Frideric Handel (1685–1759)
English Composer

Moderato

77. La Bamba

divisi, unisono, ♮

▸ Circle the notes changed by the key signature.

Mexican Folk Song

Allegro

78. Skill Builder ✓ TEST

Moderato

79. Trumpet/Cornet Private Lesson

▸ Also play this exercise on your mouthpiece alone.

MASTERING EXCELLENCE: p. 38, #4

23

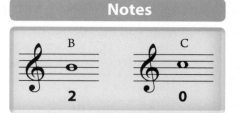

Theory & Composition

whole step – interval consisting of two half steps
major scale – series of whole (w) and half (h) steps
   in the following pattern: 1 2 3 4 5 6 7 8
   w w h w w w h
arpeggio – notes of a chord sounded one after another
orchestration – choice of instruments used to play the music

80. Going Up or Down?

81. Just By Accident

82. *Sight-Reading Challenge:*
Theme from "Orpheus In the Underworld"

In addition to composing, Jacques Offenbach was a fine cellist.

Jacques Offenbach (1819–1880)
French Composer

83. C Major Scale, Arpeggio, and Chords (Concert B♭ Major)

84. Crescent Moon Rising

Chinese Folk Song

Orchestration: Full Band — Woodwinds & Percussion — Brass & Percussion — Full Band

85. Skill Builder ✓ TEST
▶ Also play with other articulations:

Moderato

86. Excellence in Improvisation
▶ Play along with the recorded accompaniment. Measures 1-2: Play the written notes.
Measures 3-5: Improvise using

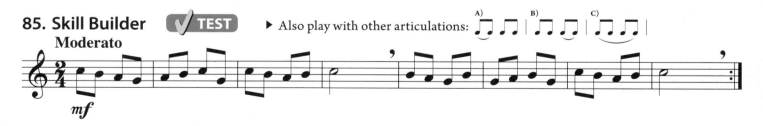

W61TP

24

Terms & Symbols		Key Signature	Notes

**sharp** – raises the pitch of a note one half step

F → F♯

courtesy accidental or **cautionary accidental** – reminder that the bar line has canceled an accidental

G major (Concert F major) – play or sing every F as F♯

F sharp (F♯)

2

#, courtesy accidental

87. Warm-up: Chop Builders
Andante
▶ Extend the 3rd valve slide to play D.
Also play this exercise on your mouthpiece alone.

88. Song of Remembrance
Moderato

89. G Major Scale, Arpeggio, and Chords (Concert F Major)
Major Scale   Arpeggio   Chords **div.**

90. Santa Lucia
▶ Circle the notes changed by the key signature.
Italian Folk Song
Moderato

91. *Sight-Reading Challenge:* Boogie Blues
Allegro

div.

92. Skill Builder ✔ TEST
Moderato

93. Trumpet/Cornet Private Lesson
▶ Repeat this exercise using the following fingerings:
0, 2, 1, 12, 23, 13, 123. Use this as a daily warm-up when you practice. Also play this exercise on your mouthpiece alone.

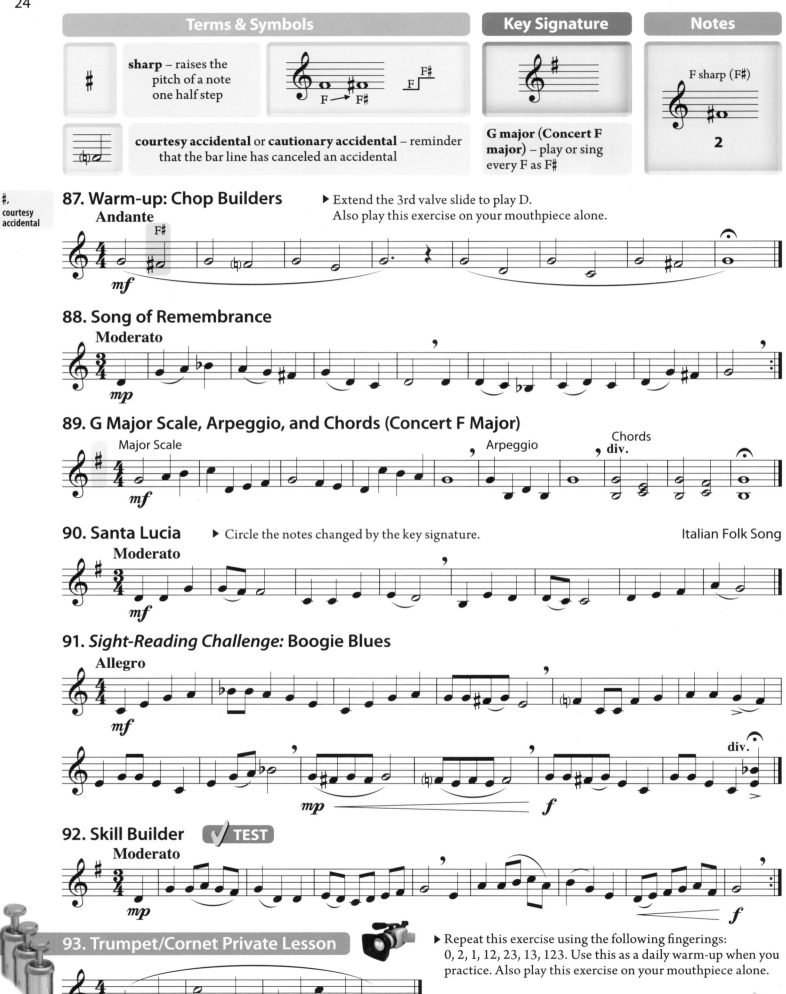

MASTERING EXCELLENCE: p. 39, #5

W61TP

Terms & Symbols

staccato – shorten the note

94. Warm-up: Tone Builder
Andante

95. F Major Scale, Arpeggio, and Chords (Concert E♭ Major)
Major Scale   Arpeggio   Chords, div.

96. When the Saints Go Marching In
When the Saints Go Marching In is often performed in a Dixieland jazz style. Dixieland originated in New Orleans, Louisiana in the early 20th century.

American Spiritual

Allegro

97. Musette
Bach's death marked the end of the Baroque Period.

Johann Sebastian Bach (1685–1750)
German Composer

Allegro   Solo/Soli   Tutti

98. Bella Bimba
Italian Folk Song

Moderato

99. Skill Builder ✓TEST
Moderato

100. Excellence in Ear Training
▶ Practice with the recorded accompaniment. Listen in measures 1, 3, 5, and 7. In measures 2, 4, 6, and 8, echo what you heard. Your starting notes are shown.

1 Listen 2 Play 3 Listen 4 Play 5 Listen 6 Play 7 Listen 8 Play

W61TP

Terms & Symbols | **Maestoso** – majestically

107. Soar!

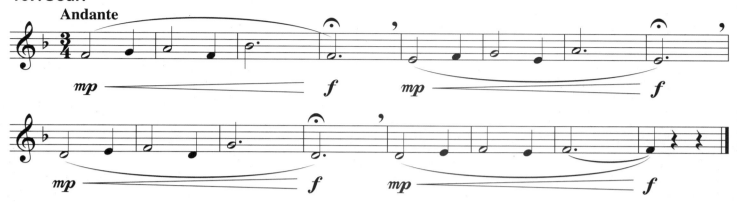

108. Skill Builder

109. *Sight-Reading Challenge:* Theme from "The Red Balloon"

▶ Extend the 3rd valve slide to play D.

Anne McGinty (b. 1945)
American Composer

From *The Red Balloon* (Q882119), ©1993 Edmondson & McGinty. All rights assigned Queenwood/Kjos 2002. Used with permission.

110. Trumpet Voluntary — *Duet* ✓ TEST

Trumpet Voluntary is also known as Prince of Denmark's March and was originally composed for harpsichord.

Jeremiah Clarke
(c. 1674–1707)
English Composer

111. Excellence in Theory ▶ Add the notes and rests together to find the number of counts. A quarter note gets one count.

Erin Watson was born in Wichita Falls, Texas, the Lone Star State. She plays violin, piano, and accordion. She studied with famed American composer Joan Tower.

118. Lone Star Waltz
▶ 1) Orchestrate by writing in the instruments that will play each two-measure section of the music. 2) Add dynamics.

Erin A. Watson (b. 1977)
American Composer

119. *Sight-Reading Challenge:* Yangtze Boatman Chantey
▶ 1) Add brackets to show the phrases. 2) Add a breath mark between the phrases.

Chinese Folk Song

120. E–Z Does It

121. Mary Ann — *Duet*
Calypso began in early 20th century Caribbean communities where slaves used music to communicate without their master's understanding. Today, the music often features guitar, steel drums, and other percussion instruments accompanying the vocals.

Calypso Song

122. Skill Builder: Happy Little Donkey — *Round* ✓TEST

American Folk Song

123. Excellence in Ear Training
▶ Practice with the recorded accompaniment. Listen in measures 1, 3, 5, and 7. In measures 2, 4, 6, and 8, echo what you heard. Your starting notes are shown.

Terms & Symbols

ritardando (*ritard.* or *rit.*) – gradually slow the tempo

Notes

124. Warm-up: Chop Builders

▶ Are you slurring with a fast and steady air stream?
Also play this exercise on your mouthpiece alone.

125. Oh Yeah!

▶ Use a focused air stream as you go up to play the D.

126. Skill Builder

127. Theme from "The Sleeping Beauty"

▶ Circle the notes changed by the key signature.

In 1891, Tchaikovsky traveled to America for the opening of Carnegie Hall in New York City.

Peter Ilyich Tchaikovsky
(1840–1893)
Russian Composer

ritardando

128. Amazing Grace ✓TEST

American Folk Song

129. Trumpet/Cornet Private Lesson

▶ Support each note with plenty of air.
▶ Increase the tempo slightly each time you practice this exercise.

MASTERING EXCELLENCE: p. 39, #7

Rhythm

syncopation – rhythmic effect that places emphasis on a weak beat

130. A Little Blue
Moderato

The blues developed in the United States during the early 1900s as an outgrowth of African-American spirituals and work songs. Blues melodies are usually 12 measures long.

131. Classical Dance
Allegro

Mozart was a child prodigy, and he traveled throughout Europe with his father to display his talents on keyboard and violin. He composed his first symphony at age 8 and his first opera at age 12.

Wolfgang Amadeus Mozart
(1756–1791)
Austrian Composer

132. Sound of Syncopation
▸ The bottom line provides the basic pulse.
Moderato

Clap

133. Sleeping Princess
Swedish Folk Song
Moderato

134. Skill Builder: Samba-lêlê ✓ TEST
Brazilian Folk Song
Moderato

135. Excellence in Theory

A. Write these tempo marks in the correct blanks: slowest ←——————————→ fastest

Andante Allegro Moderato _____ _____ _____

B. Write these dynamic marks in the correct blanks: softest ←——————————→ loudest

mf p f mp _____ _____ _____ _____

The term "military band" was historically used to designate an instrumental ensemble made up of woodwinds, brass, and percussion, much like today's concert band. **Ecossaise for Military Band** *was originally written by Beethoven in 1810 for this type of ensemble. The work is a* **contradance,** *a lively dance-inspired composition in* 2/4 *In a contradance, couples faced each other in two lines. It was a Classical Period predecessor to more modern forms such as square dancing.*

Solo: A   **Duet:** A + B   **Trio** or **Full Band:** A + B + C

Ecossaise for Military Band

▶ 1st x = first time through. 2nd x = second time through.

Ludwig van Beethoven (1770–1827)
German Composer
arr. Bruce Pearson

W61TP

BAND PIECES

Theory & Composition

ternary form – music with three sections: Section A, followed by a contrasting Section B, then Section A again

trio – third theme in a march, typically a contrasting section

Concert Etiquette

Dress nicely for every performance. If no specific guidelines are given by your director, be sure to ask what is appropriate. When you look your best, the audience will more fully appreciate your playing or singing.

ternary form

See, the Conquering Hero Comes
from "Judas Maccabaeus"

Judas Maccabaeus, composed in 1746, is one of Handel's most famous oratorios. This piece majestically commemorates the title character's victorious return from battle.

George Frideric Handel (1685–1759)
English Composer
arr. Ryan Nowlin

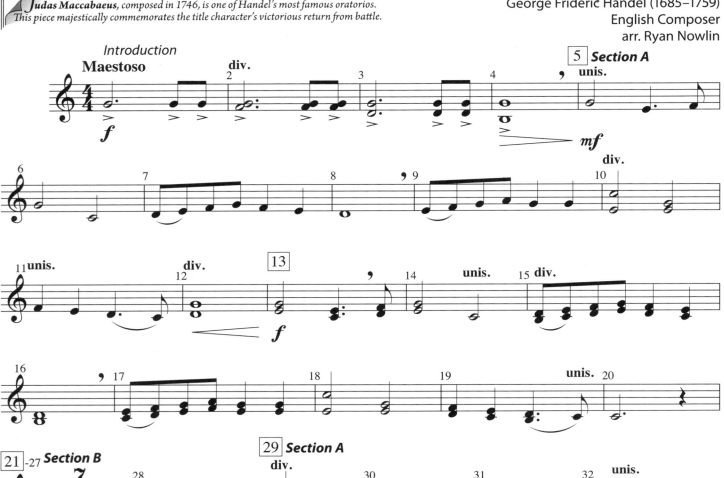

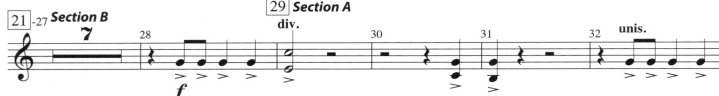

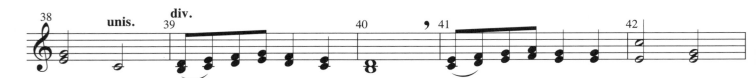

Riverside March

▶ Notice the key signature changes at 27 and 47.

trio

Ryan Nowlin (b. 1978)
American Composer

W61TP

Solo

*During the Baroque Period, virtuosic English trumpet players inspired compositions written solely for trumpet, as well as compositions for different instruments imitating the sound of a trumpet, like **Trumpet Voluntary**. For a long time, this piece was incorrectly attributed to Henry Purcell, who also wrote compositions in this style.*

Trumpet Voluntary
Solo with Piano Accompaniment

Jeremiah Clarke (c. 1674-1707)
English Composer
arr. Ryan Nowlin

MASTERING EXCELLENCE

1. After page 10, #35

Basic Preparatory Exercise

Advanced Preparatory Exercise

Mastering Excellence

2. After page 16, #60

Basic Preparatory Exercise

Advanced Preparatory Exercise

Mastering Excellence

3. After page 18, #73

Basic Preparatory Exercise

Advanced Preparatory Exercise

Mastering Excellence

4. After page 22, #79

Basic Preparatory Exercise

Advanced Preparatory Exercise

Mastering Excellence

5. After Page 24, #93

Basic Preparatory Exercise

> Repeat these exercises using the following fingerings: 0, 2, 1, 12, 23, 13, 123.
> Use these as daily warm-ups when you practice. Also play these exercises on your mouthpiece.

Advanced Preparatory Exercise

Mastering Excellence

6. After page 26, #106

Basic Preparatory Exercise

Advanced Preparatory Exercise

Mastering Excellence

7. After page 30, #129

Basic Preparatory Exercise

Advanced Preparatory Exercise

Mastering Excellence

Chop Builders

▶ Mix and match exercises 1A, 2A, and 3A in any combination.

1A.

2A.

3A.

1B, 2B, 3B. ▶ Use this line to accompany 1A, 2A, and 3A.

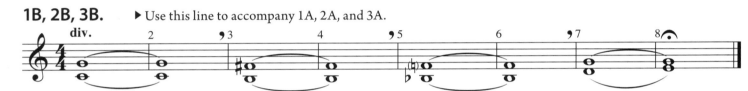

4. Match and Pass That Note

▶ Also play with other articulations:

5. Dynamic Control

C Major Warm-Up (Concert B♭ Major)

1. C Major Scale and Arpeggios

2. C Major Technique Study

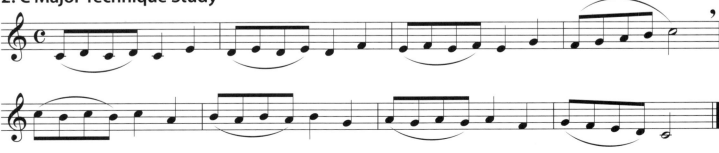

▶ Also play with other articulations:

3. C Major Balance and Tuning Study

4. C Major Chorale: All Grace and Thanksgiving

Ryan Nowlin (b. 1978)
American Composer

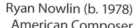

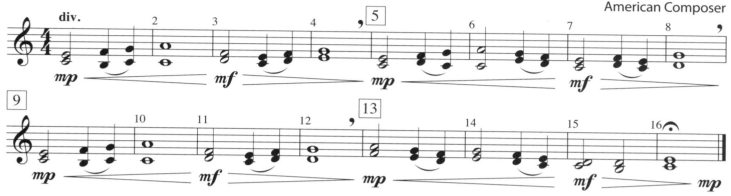

F Major Warm-Up (Concert E♭ Major)

▶ For notes you do not know, refer to the fingering chart.

1. F Major Scale and Arpeggios

2. F Major Technique Study

▶ Also play with other articulations: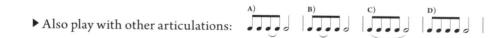

3. F Major Balance and Tuning Study

42

4. F Major Chorale: Make a Joyful Sound

Ryan Nowlin (b. 1978)
American Composer

G Major Warm-Up (Concert F Major)

▶ For notes you do not know, refer to the fingering chart.

1. G Major Scale and Arpeggios

2. G Major Technique Study

▶ Also play with other articulations:

3. G Major Balance and Tuning Study

4. G Major Chorale: Celebration and Honor

Ryan Nowlin (b. 1978)
American Composer

SCALE STUDIES

| Theory & Composition | **chromatic scale** – series of 12 ascending or descending half steps |

▶ For notes you do not know, refer to the fingering chart.

1. C Major Scale, Arpeggios, and Thirds (Concert B♭ Major)

2. F Major Scale, Arpeggios, and Thirds (Concert E♭ Major)

3. G Major Scale, Arpeggios, and Thirds (Concert F Major)

4. B♭ Major Scale, Arpeggios, and Thirds (Concert A♭ Major)

5. Chromatic Scale

W61TP

RHYTHM STUDIES

4/4 or C

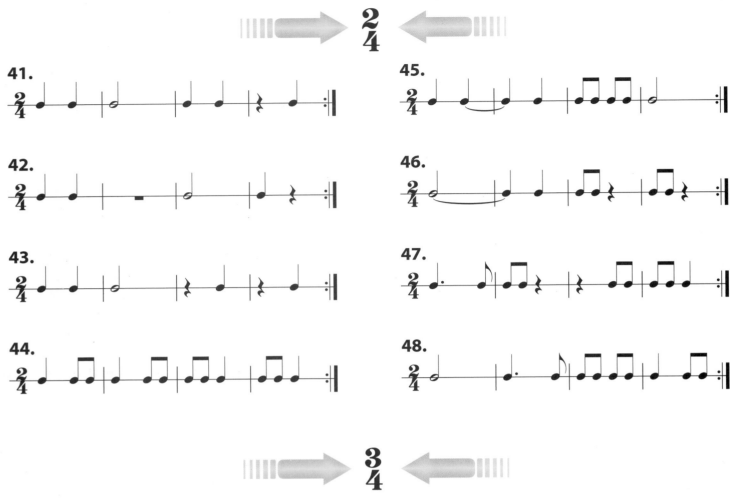

World Map

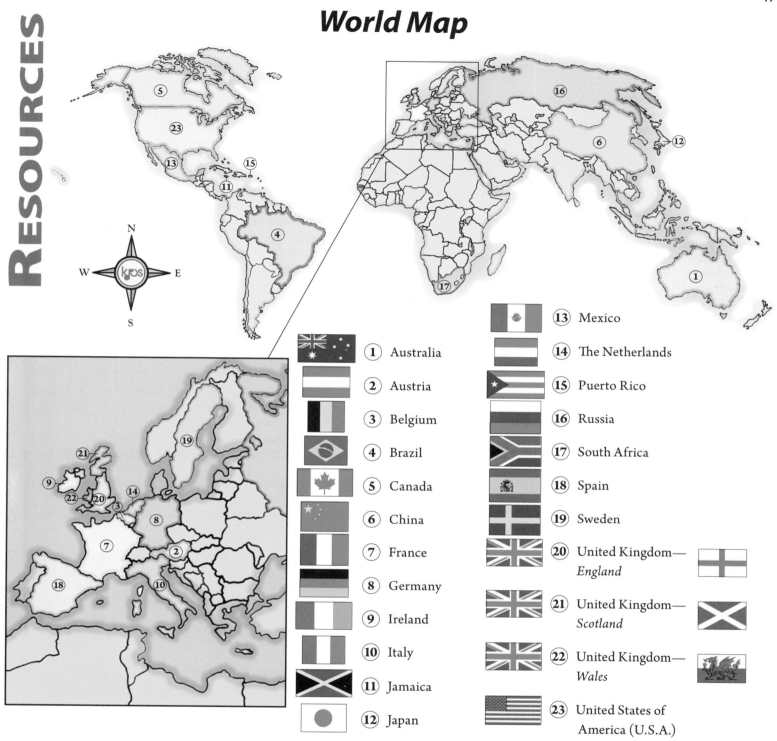

R E S O U R C E S

1	Australia	
2	Austria	
3	Belgium	
4	Brazil	
5	Canada	
6	China	
7	France	
8	Germany	
9	Ireland	
10	Italy	
11	Jamaica	
12	Japan	
13	Mexico	
14	The Netherlands	
15	Puerto Rico	
16	Russia	
17	South Africa	
18	Spain	
19	Sweden	
20	United Kingdom—*England*	
21	United Kingdom—*Scotland*	
22	United Kingdom—*Wales*	
23	United States of America (U.S.A.)	

About the Trumpet/Cornet

Trumpet History: The trumpet was used as early as 2000 BCE in China, 1500 BCE in Egypt, and 1000 BCE in Scandinavia, for the purpose of signaling and ceremonial calls. The early trumpet was long and straight with no valves. In the 14th century the trumpet was formed in a folded shape similar to today's trumpet. In the late 1700s trumpets began appearing regularly in orchestras. The valve, which was invented in 1815, allowed the trumpet to play any note of the chromatic scale.

Cornet History: The predecessor to the modern cornet was the post horn, which was a signaling instrument in the late 1500s. The instrument was lengthened over time and was used in fanfares and similar calls. Valves were added in 1828. The cornet has a mellow tone that was sought after for solos until about 1900. In 1920, the trumpet replaced the previously popular jazz cornet.

Trumpets and cornets are almost always used interchangeably in school, community, and military bands. Trumpets are also played in orchestras, jazz bands, brass ensembles, and popular music groups.

FUN FACTS

▸ Although the names are very similar, the modern cornet is not related to the medieval *cornett* or *cornetto*.

▸ The trumpet has a cylindrical bore, while the cornet has a conical bore (progressively wider toward the bell).

▸ Check out these trumpeters: Maurice Andre, Sergei Nakariakov, Adolph Herseth, Alison Balsom, Wynton Marsalis, and Susan Slaughter.

Glossary/Index

accent – (p. 18) emphasize the note

accidental – (p. 16) symbol that alters the pitch of a note until the end of the measure

Allegro – (p. 18) fast tempo

anacrusis – (p. 16) see **pick-up**

Andante – (p. 18) walking tempo; slower than **Moderato**

arpeggio – (p. 23) notes of a chord sounded one after another

articulation – (p. 10) type of attack used to play a note or group of notes

bar line – (pp. 4-6) divides the staff into measures

breath mark – (p. 7) take a breath

cautionary accidental – (p. 24) see **courtesy accidental**

chord – (p. 20) two or more notes sounded at the same time

chromatic scale – (p. 43) scale of 12 ascending or descending half steps

closing – (p. 20) last measures of a composition, often containing new material added to give a feeling of finality

common time – (p. 9) means the same as 𝄴

composition – (p. 9) creation of music that can be performed later, usually from written notation

courtesy accidental – (p. 24) reminder that the bar line has canceled an accidental

crescendo – (p. 22) gradually louder

Da Capo al Fine (*D.C. al Fine*) – (p. 26) go back to the beginning of the piece and play or sing until the *Fine*

decrescendo – (p. 22) gradually softer

Divisi (**div.**) – (p. 22) some performers play or sing the top notes while others play or sing the bottom notes

dominant – (p. 20) fifth note of a scale; chord built on the fifth note of a scale

duet – (p. 7) piece of music featuring two different parts played or sung together

dynamics – (p. 17) softness or loudness of a piece of music

embouchure – (p. 3) mouth formation used to play an instrument

fermata – (p. 12) hold a note or rest longer than its usual value

final double bar line – (pp. 4-6) marks the end of the music

1st and 2nd endings – (p. 12) play or sing the 1st ending the first time through, repeat, skip the 1st ending, and play or sing the 2nd ending

flat – (p. 16) lowers the pitch of a note one half step

forte (*f*) – (p. 17) loud

G clef – (pp. 4-6) see **treble clef**

half step – (p. 16) smallest interval used in Western music

harmony – (p. 7) two or more notes played or sung at the same time

improvisation – (p. 15) spontaneous composition of music through playing or singing

interval – (p. 16) distance between two pitches

introduction – (p. 12) opening passage of a piece of music

key signature – (p. 11) sharps or flats placed after a clef

ledger line – (pp. 4-6) short line used for notes above or below the staff

long rest – (p. 20) rest for the number of measures indicated

Maestoso – (p. 27) majestically

major scale – (p. 23) series of whole (w) and half (h) steps in the following pattern: wwhwwwh

measure – (pp. 4-6) area between two bar lines

mezzo forte (**mf**) – (p. 18) medium loud

mezzo piano (**mp**) – (p. 18) medium soft

Moderato – (p. 18) medium tempo

multiple-measure rest – (p. 20) see **long rest**

music alphabet – (pp. 4-6) first seven letters of the alphabet; these note names are assigned to the lines and spaces of the staff

natural – (p. 22) cancels a flat or sharp

one-measure repeat sign – (p. 10) play or sing the previous measure again

orchestration – (p. 23) choice of instruments used to play the music

phrase – (p. 9) musical sentence, often 4 or 8 measures long

piano (*p*) – (p. 17) soft

pick-up – (p. 16) music that comes before the first full measure of a piece

rehearsal number – (p. 12) find important places in the music using these markers

repeat sign – (p. 9) play or sing the music again

ritardando (*ritard.* or *rit.*) – (p. 30) gradually slow the tempo

round – (p. 9) song in which the same part is played or sung by two or more groups starting at different times

sharp – (p. 24) raises the pitch of a note one half step

sight-reading – (p. 7) playing or singing a piece of music for the first time

slur – (p. 10) articulation that connects notes of *different* pitches; indicates a very smooth sound

Soli – (p. 9) a small group or section plays or sings

Solo – (p. 9) only one person plays or sings

staccato – (p. 25) shorten the note

staff – (pp. 4-6) 5 lines and 4 spaces for writing music

subdominant – (p. 20) fourth note of a scale; chord built on the fourth note of a scale

syncopation – (p. 31) rhythmic effect that places emphasis on a weak beat

tempo – (p. 18) speed of a piece of music

ternary form – (p. 34) music with three sections: Section A, followed by a contrasting Section B, then Section A again

theme – (p. 12) a melody within a piece of music

theme and variation – (p. 16) type of composition that begins with a main melody (**theme**) and continues with different versions (**variations**) of the main melody

tie – (p. 11) marking that connects notes of the *same* pitch to make one longer note

time signature – (pp. 4-6) top number tells you the number of counts per measure; bottom number tells you the type of note that gets one count

tonic – (p. 20) first note of a scale; chord built on the first note of a scale

treble clef – (pp. 4-6) the line it circles on the staff is called **G**

trio (ensemble) – (p. 12) piece of music featuring three different parts played or sung together

trio (march) – (p. 34) third theme in a march, typically a contrasting section

Tutti – (p. 9) everyone plays or sings

unisono (*unis.*) – (p. 22) everyone plays or sings the same notes

variation – (p. 16) see **theme and variation**

whole step – (p. 23) interval consisting of two half steps

Timeline

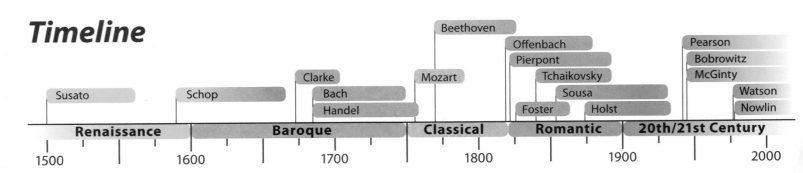